Rahel Lämmler and Michael Wagner

in collaboration with the
Müther Archive of the College of Wismar

Ulrich Müther Shell Structures

in Mecklenburg-Western Pomerania

Niggli

Table of Contents

Nimble Ease

Between State Purposes and Architectural Experiment

Strolling east along the beach at Binz, one comes upon the lifeguard rescue tower, built in 1981. The white painted concrete shell floats above the dunes as if it had come from another planet. In actuality, however, it is the second of its kind. Its predecessor, completed in 1975, stood only 500 meters away, where the main road dead-ends at the beach. In 1993, when the former pier was rebuilt on axis with the road, the older rescue tower was displaced and demolished without a second thought to make space for it. Many buildings by the Binz engineer Ulrich Müther have already suffered this fate.

The white "UFO" was one of our first discoveries on Rügen; it provided our initial access to an extraordinary, if ambivalent, chapter in German architectural history. The astonishing amalgam of form and function inspired us to search out the clever mind behind the bold construction. By then, however, Ulrich Müther was already acutely ill. His wife, Astrid von Zydowitz-Müther permitted us access to an oeuvre, which without doubt encompasses some of the jewels of former East Germany's architectural heritage.

In the years immediately after the realization of his thesis project of 1963 (see page 40), Müther was able to build an impressive number of so-called hyperbolic shells in quick succession.

His expressive shell roofs struck the nerve of that era. Only a few centimeters thick, the concrete shells span large, column-free spaces; fascinating in their exceptionality, they offered a tangible image for oft-invoked progress. Most often, they were deployed for highly noticeable, freestanding public buildings.

After an optimistic transitional phase in the 1960s, the majority of the following decades' architectural production in the GDR did not live up to the high expectations. Enthusiasm for innovation in the area of housing, initially admired internationally, gave way to stereotypical industrial production, which left little room for planners to experiment. Many discouraged architects and engineers emigrated to West Germany. Those who remained sought out niches for themselves. Thus, by focusing on "special concrete buildings," Ulrich Müther was able to realize his engineering dreams working with like-minded collaborators. The integration of architects, engineers and other construction specialists in his office made it possible to

2

create architecture that in a way exceeded the usual limitations. Müther's vibrant shell forms and their ingenious construction embodied the exact opposite of the dominant East German elemental construction ("Plattenbauweise") and was a welcome exception to the average grey-tone of GDR architecture. Although they are among the most significant witnesses to this chapter of architecture history, his structures are only known in small professional circles.

Functional demands were transformed by the political shifts of 1989, so that many of his buildings are now disused, empty or decrepit. Many have been renovated since reunification, but unfortunately often without sensitivity. This represents a huge challenge for preservationists. From their perspective, continuity of use is an integral component for insuring the sustainable preservation of worthy buildings. Owners, investors, government officials and architects must offer adequate solutions.

2000 saw the demolition of the Ahornblatt (maple leaf) in Berlin, only shortly prior to greater media attention. With the destruction of this 1973 cafeteria for the GDR's Ministry of Building, the city lost a symbolic icon. This event triggered a heated discussion about the preservation of buildings from the recent past, positioning Müther in the sightlines of architects and engineers.

With the exception of Wilfried Dechau's out-of-print publication *Kühne Solitäre* ("Bold Stand-Alones"), published in 2000 as part of the book series put out by the journal *deutsche bauzeitung*, Müther's work has only been marginally received. In recent years, summary articles and brief descriptions of singular buildings have appeared in newspapers and magazines. There is still nothing, which offers a representative overview of all the shell structures with drawings, contemporary photographs and surviving architecture historic material.

4

Because of changed conditions, shell construction is only seldom used today because the production of formwork is difficult and time-intensive. The cost of labor has become far too high relative to that of material. Only an enormous reduction in production time and difficulty, for example through prefabrication of shell elements, could achieve a rational construction process. The sustainability of shell structures also remains an unsolved problem. In the 1960s and 1970s, the surfaces of the shells were only minimally insulated and windows were only single-glazed. There is still no answer to the problem of how to achieve contemporary energy performance in a filigree shell construction. A critical reception of this nearly forgotten construction technology coupled with new approaches to construction could contribute to the revitalization of shell structures. Even beyond the need to answer technically solvable questions, architects and engineers are confronted with the challenge of developing together a contemporary formal language based upon high structural performance, growing ecological demands and the use of new technologies. This could result in buildings and spaces whose significance points beyond the merely contemporary.

This guidebook is a first step towards making Müther's shell structure technique in its entirety available to an interested audience and towards generating sensitivity towards the existing substance and cultural heritage of the GDR. Müther's shell constructions can best be discovered naturally, onsite. His floating parabolic shells reward those who seek them out with an unaccustomed modern aesthetic pleasure and suggest the euphoria and belief in progress that characterized the time of their formation.

Rahel Lämmler and Michael Wagner

Rahel Lämmler and Michael Wagner received their degrees at the Department of Architecture of the ETH in Zurich. They live and work in Zurich.

1 Restaurant Inselparadies, Baabe, 1966
2 Restaurant Kosmos, Rostock Südstadt, 1970
3 Municipal Hall Neubrandenburg, 1968
4 Vacationers' Restaurant Szczecin, Binz, 1978

Ulrich Müther's Hypar Shells

Grace and Elegance in Concrete

Almost no one is immune to the fascination of the double curved shell. Architects are seduced by their uplift and lightness. Civil engineers admire the logical flow of force lines along their forms. Mathematicians are perhaps reminded of lectures on geometry, and the singular position of hyperbolic paraboloid shells in the spectrum bounded at either end by simplicity and complexity. Laypersons simply see the beauty of these seemingly levitating roofs; it is precisely this apparently naïve sense of wonder that comes closest to their builders' desire.

It seems almost as though Ulrich Müther began with the viewpoint of a layperson and maintained it for his entire life. Whilst achieving a high level of technical and formal precision in his work, he still pursued the goal of realizing a beautiful building. Ulrich Müther was a structural engineer. Society's reception of him is nonetheless denoted by the title of architect so often, although incorrectly, lent to him. Ulrich Müther, on the other hand, liked to call himself a provincial master builder, or a master builder of shells. This fine sense of irony, typical of the coastal North, also bespeaks his well-developed self-confidence. The concept of "master builder" derives its reputation from a centuries-old tradition stretching from the Gothic to the Modern era. Master builders were and are – in the Alpine republics, for example, it is still a legally regulated professional title – often craftsmen with an extended, in some cases academic, education. Above all, however, they are both planners and executors of buildings. Ulrich Müther realized his concrete shells as a *Gesamtkunstwerk*: he researched them through experimentation, projected them mathematically, designed them architecturally, calculated them as an engineer, assessed them as a salesman and built them as a craftsman. This differentiates him from other engineers who worked with double-curved concrete shells, such as the Swiss Heinz Isler (1926–2009) or the Italian Pier Luigi Nervi (1891–1979), who left the actual construction to others. Ulrich Müther was an entrepreneur in all things related to shell building, and managed to assume that role even in socialist Germany. Many of the shell structures collected in this book are hyperbolic paraboloids (called "hypar shells"). Their name and their form derive from a plane against which a conceptual parabola has been slipped along a hyperbola

1

to create a secondary curvature. As complex as this imaginary action in space may seem, it has one astonishing characteristic: it can as easily be accomplished using a series of simple straight lines. If one subdivides two non-parallel lines equally, then connects the points of subdivision with another straight line, the resulting plane is also a hyperbolic paraboloid. This method of creating a hypar shell can be seen in every old city in Europe: if the peak of the roof and the cornice line (or gutter) are not parallel, then the framing that connects them forms a curved plane. The hypar plane can thus also be created from straight lines; but nonetheless, it is upon completion a so-called non-developable surface. Unlike a cone but exactly like a sphere, it cannot be modeled from a single sheet of paper. Surfaces such as these have special qualities, which means that their very high structural stability despite minimal material thickness can be of use to the builder of a soccer ball, a hi-fi speaker membrane or, as in our case, a concrete shell.

The material plays as important a role as the geometry. The particular nature of reinforced concrete as a hybrid material derives from the synergy between the two component materials. Whereas concrete is very strong in compression but cannot withstand tension, the thin steel bars of the reinforcing have exactly the opposite qualities. The fact that both share an almost equivalent coefficient of thermal expansion makes them perfect partners for a lifetime. In the concrete shells, there are additional advantages at play: the reinforcing can at least in part follow the straight lines, which stretch between the two inclined edges. Concrete, on the other hand, is viscous during construction, and thus fulfills the basic requirement for a non-developable surface. By comparison, shell structures in steel sheeting are geometrically impossible and those built in wood cannot achieve full surface bearing capacity and are therefore statically inefficient. This is also the reason that shell structures such as those by German shell structure pioneer Franz Dischinger were realized, alongside flat plates and straight columns, even in early reinforced concrete building. These kinds of bearing structures exploit all the advantages of reinforced concrete and avoid its disadvantages, particularly its considerable material weight.

To build a shell, one needs a formwork on top of which the viscous concrete can cure before it has achieved its bearing capacity. These kinds of formworks were, throughout the 1960s, usually built from rough-cut pine boards nailed to end beams. The enormous weight of the concrete demanded a veritable forest of columns beneath the formwork as well as numerous horizontal springing points and cross-braces. Because this construc-

tion was built by hand from wooden beams and boards, naturally a hypar shell could be realized as easily by positioning two edge beams askew to each other before the intermediary boards were nailed in place.

The disappearance of these kinds of shells in

the early 1970s goes hand in hand with the rationalization of concrete building. In the era of mass housing, Western European countries focused on large-plate formwork elements such as those which are now seen without exception at construction sites; in Eastern Europe, the emphasis was on prefabricated panel construction. In the shortest time imaginable, both techniques had marginalized the much more labor-intensive board formwork and with it, shell construction. Shell construction today is not technically, but rather only economically obsolete.

To cast concrete on a steeply sloped surface is, naturally, not easy. A concrete mix that is too liquid slips off but a mix that is too stiff will form too many air bubbles and lose bearing capacity. Ulrich Müther and his long-time staff used gunite, also called shotcrete, a technique known since the 1920s. In this technique, the dry cement/sand mixture is shot under high pressure from a hose at the end of which a second hose adds precisely the right amount of water. This method demands not only a sophisti-

cated pumping technology but also a high level of technical skill in order to add the water correctly. The fact that Ulrich Müther's company VEB Spezialbetonbau (Special Concrete Building) Rügen could insure both the planning and the execution of these kinds of

3

buildings translated into commissions for shell roofs in the GDR as well as for luge and bobsled run, cycling tracks or planetaria in other socialist and Western countries.

Even today, Ulrich Müther's buildings have not lost any of their fascination, and little of their substance. Even in cases where the architecture beneath the shells is in disrepair or destroyed, the concrete shells demonstrate their impressive powers of resistance even against the aggressive Baltic Sea climate. Rather, they are only threatened by economic pressure and hydraulic hammers. All that can protect them is wide social acceptance: not as 'Ostalgia' but rather as witnesses to a bygone and irrevocable building technology whose entire beauty derives from lightness which at the time was entirely new and even today, seems outrageous.

Georg Giebeler

Prof. of Architecture Georg Giebeler is Professor for Building Construction and Dean of the Division of Design at the College of Wismar. He is the director of the Müther Archives.

The large restaurant Ahornblatt, Berlin, 1973:
1 after the assembly of the shell
2 formwork
3 execution of the gunite

Concrete Shell Structures

An historical perspective

The fascination of spanning great dimensions using only minimal material has always been a driving force for technological development in building construction. In the case of shell buildings, efficiency and structural capacity are created by a correctly chosen form through which, at least in terms of material dead weight, pure membrane action results (in compression and tension) for the supporting structure and thus allows for the material used to be minimized. The nearly unlimited plastic formability of fresh concrete which can be cast in forms, troweled over surfaces with any desired curvature or sprayed on makes it the ideal material for this kind of construction. Integral, at best pre-tensioned reinforcement gives the shell its strength in tension. Thanks to prefabrication, quality and economy can be increased.

Long-span thin-shell concrete structures were invented around 1920, when concrete construction was still young. They first took the form of barrel vaults and domes, and thereafter were realized in other mathematical, rotationally symmetrical planes. Concrete shells offered an interesting alternative to lightweight steel construction and to reinforced concrete domes with solid bearing ribs. As early as 1923, Eugène Freyssinet (1879–1962) built the airport hangars at Orly using undulating shells spanning 75 meters. In Germany, the production and measurement processes for shell structures were developed by Ulrich Finsterwalder (1897-1988) and Franz Dischinger (1887–1953) for Dyckerhoff & Widmann AG and by Walther Bauersfeld (1879-1959) for Carl Zeiss Jena, among others. This development is evidenced by a number of surprising, smaller experimental buildings, such as the barely two centimeter thick domed shell at Dyckerhoff & Widmann AG in Jena of 1932, as well as larger domed buildings, such as the Zeiss Planetarium in Jena, spanning 24.8 meters and built by the same firm in 1926 (illustration 1). In the case of the planetarium, gunite (shotcrete) technology was used, allowing for the rational realization of steeply sloped shell surfaces even above the workers' heads. As an alternative, thin shells could also be realized by troweling a fine layer of mortar onto a supporting cage of reinforcing wires or mesh. Depending on the technique used, the

1

2

reinforcing could entirely substitute for the formwork itself as with Ferrocemento developed by Pier Luigi Nervi.

In the 1930s, the sculptural capacities of reinforced concrete were more thoroughly exploited thanks to continued experimentation in model and test structures. Shell forms during this period focused on geometric, mathematically describable surfaces. In addition to domed and conical forms, design work also included shells with oposing curvatures such as hyperbolic paraboloids, for example Giorgio Baroni's folded plate roofs realized in 1938 in Milan and in 1939 in Ferrara. For bearing structures using linear elements, generally accepted calculation methods had been developed and codified into norms. In the case of shell structures, however, the field was still open. For this type of bearing structures, typical membrane theory, according to which the state of equilibrium in horizontals and meridians is reached by equally distributed loading was no longer adequate. Along the edges of the shell, this creates a bending stress, which is necessary to maintain equilibrium. This meant that new means had to be developed in order to study and master the structural behavior and stability of such thin shells. The Spanish engineer, builder and academic Eduardo Torroja (1899–1961) pursued one possible method of studying and predicting systematically structural behavior using scientifically planned experiments on scaled models. In his point-supported thin-shell dome incorporating a pre-tensioned ring beam for a market hall in Algeciras of 1934 (illustration 2) and in his roof for the spectator stands at the horse race track La Zarzuela in Madrid, also of 1938 (illustration 3), Torroja demonstrated impressively the potentials which a fully consistent use of prestressed reinforced concrete technologies and model testing can open up for shell structures. Nervi, too, ran similar experiments for his 1938 cross rib vault reinforced concrete airport hangar in Orvieto.

In modern post-war shell construction, the tactical use of model analysis proved indispensable. Several former students of Edu-

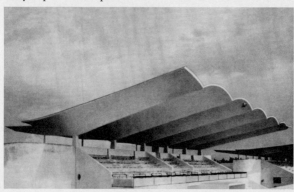

3

ardo Torroja, including his son Juan Antonio Torroja (*1933) and Heinz Hossdorf (1925–2006), made essential contributions to the further development of this design and calculation method. Using pre-tensioning, long-span suspended shells could also be realized. Ulrich Finsterwalder's highly respected Schwarzwald Hall in Karlsruhe of 1954, spanning between 73 and 48 meters with a mere 6 centimeter thickness, is the first German example of this technique.

In the 1950s and early 1960s, shell construction experienced its high point at an international scale. Simultaneous with the full development of the formal potentials inherent to reinforced concrete, new methods of form finding were also used. Because it is only possible to realize that which can be statically determined and measured, methods for calculating the statics of shells were developed further and were soon supported by computers.

As part of this development, the International Association for Shell and Spatial Structures (IASS) made an essential contribution to supporting and disseminating knowledge on shell building beyond national boundaries and the Iron Curtain. On the invitation of Eduardo Torroja, whose authority and pioneering work especially in shell building was undeniable, an international group of engineers met in Madrid in 1959 to found the Association. These included the most famous shell builders of the time, such as Nicolas Esquillan (1902–1989), Félix Candela (1910–1997) and Ove Arup (1895–1988). The IASS set itself the goal of supporting progressive developments in the design and realization of shells, later to include all spatial structures, on an international scale. Without doubt, they achieved their goal: the congresses' records represent a very respectable register of the latest developments. The IASS was consistent in its attempts to assert itself beyond the boundaries of world politics and to be present above all in Eastern Europe. Such superb shell builders as Félix Candela held lectures, also in the GDR, where Hermann Rühle, Vicepresident of the IASS and later honorary member, did much to maintain international contacts. Within the area of new surface structures beyond those described by mathematical functions, the form-finding and oeuvre of Heinz Isler has primary importance. In 1959 at the first IASS congress, Isler gave a short presentation entitled *Neue Formen für Schalen* (New Shapes for Shells). Isler had developed three different methods for shell building: the suspension method (using suspended reinforcing cloth without intermediary supports that was then solidified), the flow method (extrusion of a viscous mass over an opening) and the pneumatic method (inflation of a bubble whose edges are held in place in a frame). The forms produced by these experiments were optimized using precise modeling and model-based experimentation to insure that the shells' dead weight was only strained by membrane action. Isler's designs were based upon one single tenet: unlike the case of trabeated structures, there is no *single* efficient form for shells in which loading is purely carried by compressive or tensile forces (the line of force relative to a link or funicular polygon). Rather, there are many conceivable geometries, which distribute load so that the shell can carry it in a way appropriate to membrane action, without creating bending stress. The converse is also true, that a certain form of shell can carry several configurations of distributed loads by means of membrane action. Isler's active search for an efficient rather than geometric form (to speak in his terms) led on the one hand to new shell constructions, which, in such cases as a shallow domed shell, became economically viable in a serial array. On the other hand, free organic forms with a high degree of formal expression were now also imaginable, especially for freestanding shell buildings (illustration 4).

Ulrich Müther's engineering studies and the beginning of his professional life were simultaneous with precisely these break-through years in the construction of concrete shells. The developments and innovations in calculation and construction techniques were well known to him and other shell builders in Eastern Europe. During stays in Budapest and Leningrad in 1966 and upon Jörg Schlaich's invitation to Stuttgart in 1968, Müther established international relationships. His intertwining of theory and practice, of laboratory experiment, the necessity for dimentioning and the optimization of construction methods, is typical of shell building in those years. In order to verify the bearing performance of his shells, he relied upon tests done on models or on the buildings themselves. He undertook elaborate computer-aided statistical studies in collaboration with various academic institutions. His collaboration with his thesis professor Reinhold Rabich (1902–1974) proved extremely valuable in this regard. As an entrepreneur, Müther could, finally, directly influence the quality of construction by training his specialized workers and by constantly adjusting the process of building. In the process, he could deploy the experience gathered for new approaches to his work.

Müther's experiments with unusual forms and construction techniques, which he used to avoid costly formwork, are particularly apparent in his small buildings: for the lifeguard rescue tower in Binz, he cast the shell components on hills made of sand (see page 44). This is a method that for example Nervi, too, used repeatedly to prefabricate shell elements. The small funnel-shaped shell for the book kiosk in Baabe (see page 54) and the Kurmuschel (concert shell) in Sassnitz (see page 60) are also worth noting for their form. His most formally daring design is, however, the 1977 freely-formed suspended shell used to roof the swimming pool at the ZK-vacation community near Sellin (see page 50). There, the tensional forces are anchored in the opposing perimeter beams and thus brought into equilibrium. The shell was studied at the Institute for Ship Building in Rostock using a computer model with finite elements.

5

In addition to the various ways of finding form, the composition of shell structures with the same basic form also offers a nearly inexhaustible source of variation. The work of the Spanish engineer and contractor Félix Candela in Mexico proves the architectural potential of this way of working. He derived the form and aesthetic expression of many of his buildings from a combination of hypar shells. As an advantage to its production, this form of shell can be made with the formwork boards arrayed along its generative straight lines. Moreover, stresses can be measured using commensurate efforts in calculation. The parameters for the composition derive from the orientation of the elements in space, their folds along their shared edges, the configuration of the free edges and the integration of façade elements with which the bearing structure is stabilized.

Candela's early work was superbly documented in 1963 by Colin Faber in his publication *Candela – The Shell Builder*. It is clear that his influence inspired Müther's work. Beginning with his first shell, which he realized for the roof of the multipurpose room in the House of the Steel Workers in Binz in 1963 (see page 40), Müther built a considerable number of folded roofs comprising hypar shells. The way in which the shell's free edges were stabilized became, over time, more elegant or disappeared altogether. In the case of the shallow shell modules with rectangular plans, made up of hypar planes and arrayed serially to roof larger spaces, Candela's work – for example, the Rio warehouse from 1954 in Mexico City – also offered important precedents for roof form and static analysis. His design for the columns in the 1955 Church of the Miraculous Virgin in Mexico City (illustration 5), for example, seem to have influenced Müther's work for the cafeteria at the Wismar Engineering College (see page 96).

In Müther's most representative projects, too, Candela's influence is easily recognizable: for the convention center (see page 74) and the Kosmos restaurant (see page 82) in Rostock, the row of shell elements are supported along their shared edge and are respectively shifted against one another in their height and orientation. Candela used a similar compositional principle for the beach club at the Playa Azul of 1958 (illustration 6). In the innovative shell for the nightclub La Jacaranda in Acapulco from 1957, three hypar planes with curved free edges give the impression of intertwining leaves whose intersecting curves resolve into the shell's three points of support. This project can be understood as the source of inspiration for Müther's elegant shell for the Teepott restaurant in Warnemünde (see page 88). The form of the Seerose restaurant in Potsdam (see page

110) with its shells all arranged radial symmetrically in plan, was based upon Candela's 1958 restaurant Los Manantiales in Xochimilco. In the Neubrandenburg city hall of 1968 (see page 100), the hypar shells are arranged symmetrically around a zenithal opening and tensioned together. The bearing structure recalls that of Candela's 1960 Church of San José Obrero in Monterrey (illustration 7), in which the façade columns are tightened down to stabilize the shell. Müther in fact used the church's stylized form for his company logo (see page 33).

Many of Müther's shells were built in the second half of the 1960s and in the 1970s, at a time when the largest wave of concrete shell building had crested, at least in Western Europe. It was not only the high cost of formwork in comparison to labor costs that led to the decline in shell construction. The interest of engineers, architects and technicians slowly shifted to new materials and systems: long-span roofs could increasingly be realized in glass, plexiglass or textile membrane or other tensile

6

structural systems, as was done impressively, for example, for the sports buildings at the Olympia Park in Munich from 1972 by Frei Otto and Behnisch & Partner Architekten. These kinds of construction techniques could produce well-lit spaces whose shells were designed to be seen as glowing volumes from the exterior. The construction methods involved in realizing these suspension cable-based structures are more modest than those used for shells; cable structures can also, if needed, be raised, taken apart and used again for temporary uses. The development of computer-aided statics and the associated increase in calculation and modeling capacity offers superb tools for the design of geometrically complex bearing structures today. Thanks to technical developments in production technologies, building components with complex forms, also, for example, in wood, can be precisely fabricated. And nonetheless, there has been no renaissance in shell building.

The increasingly all-encompassing use of computer programs in the design process has, in contrast to the era of the model, led to the quick acceptance of certain a priori conceptions of a "free form" which can then, thanks to the available means, be digitalized, calculated and realized rather than a process in which the form is produced and optimized relative to static efficiency. As a result, shell surfaces are often built which are not often carried by shell structural action. Continuing interest in shell forms is unfortunately countered by the fact that static efficiency is not always the decisive criterion for the production of form. The deployment of digital design tools, which at least in part replace experimentation with models, does not, how-

7

ever, produce an increase in the expressive power or formal quality of bearing structures. As always, the structure is essentially
dependent upon conceptual design work and results from the
combination of the author's sensitivity to form and statics. This
mastery results from direct experimentation with form and bearing structure. In this spirit, a return to craft would be desirable.

Massimo Laffranchi

Dr. Massimo Laffranchi is professor at the Accademia di architettura in Mendrisio and a board member of the Society for Civil Engineering. He is an associate of the engineering firm of Fürst Laffranchi in Wolfwil (Switzerland).

1 Zeiss Planetarium, Jena, Germany, 1926; Ulrich Finsterwalder, Franz Dischinger, Walter Bauersfeld
2 Market Hall, Algeciras, Spain, 1934; Manuel Sánchez Arcas, Eduardo Torroja
3 Roof for the spectators stand at La Zarzuela horse racing track, Madrid, Spain, 1935–1941; Carlos Arniches, Martín Domínguez, Eduardo Torroja
4 Garden Center Carlo Bürgi, Camorino, Switzerland, 1973; Heinz Isler
5 Church of La Virgen Milagrosa, Narvarte, Mexico, 1955; Félix Candela
6 Beach club, Playa Azul, Venezuela, 1958; Guillermo Shelley, José Chavez, Félix Candela
7 Church of San José Obrero, Monterrey, Nuevo Leon, Mexiko, 1960; Enrique de la Mora y Palomar, Félix Candela

Biography
Ulrich Müther (1934–2007)

At the time of Ulrich Müther's birth on July 21, 1934 in Binz on the island of Rügen, his parents had been running the building firm Baugeschäft Willy Müther for twelve years. Upon his father's death in 1947 his mother Elisabeth Müther continues to direct the firm alone. A few years later, she marries the master builder August Keller, who then assumes direction of the firm.

After World War II, as the son of self-employed parents in the GDR, Ulrich Müther is denied the direct route to enter an academic high school and to conduct studies at a university. After elementary school, he therefore decides to train as a carpenter and thereafter adds another year as a journeyman. At the age of 17, Müther begins his studies at the engineering school in Neustrelitz where he acquires initial knowledge of statics and engineering.

After his studies end in 1954, Müther spends four years planning power plants in the Design Office for Industrial Building in the Berlin Ministry for Construction. Simultaneously, he begins a correspondence course in 1956 in civil engineering at the Technical University of Dresden (then called the Technical College of Dresden).

In the meantime, the new political situation has created pressures which drastically change the circumstances in Binz: in the aftermath of the "Aktion Rose", the Müther family is briefly dispossessed in February 1953, but then regains control of their building firm after the popular revolt of June 17, 1953 and continues its direction of the firm under new regulations. While taking his correspondence course, Ulrich Müther assumes the technical directorship of his family's company at the end of 1958, which the East German state restructures in 1960 as a trade-based production combine with the name PGH Bau Binz. At the Professorship for Theory and Construction of Planar Bearing Structures under Professor Reinhold Rabich, Müther focuses on concrete shell construction. His 1963 thesis project for a gunite hypar shell with double curvature marks the end of his studies in Dresden. In the same year, he builds his final project as the roof for a multi-purpose space in the vacation hotel House of the Steel Workers in Binz (see page 40). This is considered the first reinforced concrete hypar shell in the GDR. During his studies, Müther had met Hermann Rühle, who

1

was a research assistant at the Professorship for Reinforced Concrete and Monolithic Bridge Construction. In 1966, through Rühle's connections, he travels to the building exposition in Budapest, where he meets such other famous shell builders as Jörg Schlaich (*1934), Stefan Polónyi (*1930) and Heinz Isler (1926–2009). He also attends the 1966 IASS (International Association for Shell and Spatial Structures) convention in Leningrad.

Müther is fascinated by the potentials of shell building: he starts collecting empirical knowledge for further projects by means of small-scale test shells at home in Binz. The influential concrete shells realized by the Spanish engineer Félix Candela (1910–1997) in Mexico leave their mark on his experiments.

In the same year, Müther sets the foundation for his future success with the construction of his building for the Baltic Sea convention center in Rostock Schutow (see page 74) and attracts the attention of East German professional circles. Upon the convention center's completion, this interest leads to commissions for several restaurants using hypar shells.

Erich Kaufmann (1932–2004), who designed the convention center with Müther, is one of the primary architects within the Rostock housing combine. He includes Müther's shell constructions in multiple projects although the official government planning office employs many architects and engineers and enjoys a near-monopoly on larger building projects in Rostock and environs. For all new residential areas from about 1965 on, the planners design so-called compact buildings or community centers with which to satisfy "material and cultural needs." Müther's hypar shells are deployed in several buildings of this type (see pages 78, 92, 96).

In 1972, PGH Bau Binz is taken over by the State and transformed into a State-owned company ('Volkseigener Betrieb' or VEB). Although the structure of the VEB Spezialbetonbau Rügen does not allow for his prior independence, the State take-over proves Müther's advantage: because of its focus on special types of concrete construction, the firm assumes an almost unchallenged position in the GDR outside of the combines. Although Müther is not a party member, the political leadership welcomes his shell structures as innovative and exemplary projects. They insure international recognition for the young country. With his staff of on occasion numbering more than 100 employees, Müther is able not only to plan and calculate buildings but also to realize them efficiently. First in his role as the director of the PGH and later of the VEB, Müther realizes a large number of buildings.

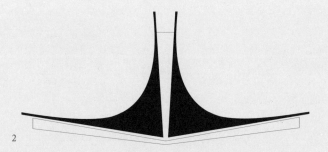

By virtue of his concrete shells, he is primarily active in the area of so-called special buildings: beginning in the 1960s, he is responsible for restaurants, pavilions, gyms and church buildings in his native region and throughout the GDR. Müther's shell structures lend new socialist Germany of the 1960s and 1970s an ideal architectural radiance with which to define itself against West Germany. The minimal use of materials, which were in short supply anyway, was perfectly suited to the context of the general move towards rationalized building.

In 1989, his son dies from an asthma attack. Müther's response to his loss is the founding of the Christian Müther Foundation, through which he conducts annual sailing trips in the waters around Rügen with prominent sailors and some 300 sick children.

After German reunification, the family business is returned to Müther in 1990 and renamed Müther GmbH Spezialbetonbau (special concrete building). Müther is involved for six

3

years as the president of the Mecklenburg-Western Pomeranian Association of the Building Industry. He continues his work without interruption but the situation has changed with the introduction of the free market economy: in 1999, at the age of 65, Müther is forced to declare bankruptcy.

Ulrich Müther realizes more than sixty shell structures in his 36 years of professional practice. His pioneering constructions are built on the island of Rügen, in and around Rostock and in the larger Mecklenburg-Western Pomerania region. His international collaboration with the firm of Carl Zeiss Jena, beginning with the construction of the Spacemaster planetarium in Tripoli (Libya), and his various racetracks in Germany and worldwide comprise another significant portion of his work (see pages 112–113).

Within the discipline, a new reception of his work begins with the turn of the century, and he is increasingly often invited to congresses and conventions. The demolition of the Berlin Ahornblatt (Maple Leaf) in August of 2000 was above all responsible for making this previously little-acknowledged engineer better known in architectural and engineering circles. In that same year, Müther begins to organize and collect his project archives. Since 2006, all this material in the form of drawings, models and documents is administered at the College of Wismar as the Müther Archives. After a long illness, Ulrich Müther dies on August 21, 2007, in Binz, Rügen.

1 Ulrich Müther (in the middle)
2 Logo of the VEB Spezialbetonbau Rügen
3 The Spacemaster Planetarium in Tripoli, Libya, 1981

Ulrich Müther Shell Structures

in Mecklenburg-Western Pomerania

The Island of Rügen

Multi-Purpose Space for the Haus der Stahlwerker (House of the Steel Workers)

Construction roof surface of four hypar shells on corner posts, 14.2 x 14.2 m, shell thickness 7 cm Use multi-purpose space Status demolished 2002 Address Zeppelinstraße 8, 18609 Ostseebad Binz

1964 The Four Seasons Hotel is located in the center of Binz, parallel to the main thoroughfare. In the dining room space where luxurious meals are now served, GDR steel workers from the Riesa rolling mill used to spend their company holidays. Ulrich Müther designed, calculated and built four hypar surfaces above a square plan for the roof of the former multi-purpose space to extend an existing single-floor annex. The roof was also Müther's diploma thesis, on the basis of which he completed after seven years his correspondence course at the TU Dresden with Professor Reinhold Rabich in 1963. In the same year, the building's structural frame was completed, and in 1964, the dining room opened. This roof is considered the first hypar shell construction in reinforced concrete in the GDR. In addition to Müther's own computations for the bearing shell structure, the load distribution was tested by the TU Dresden using a plaster model. The roof was placed on the corner posts, with the vertical window frames serving solely as additional stiffening. Since German reunification, the hotel used the former multi-purpose space as breakfast room. In the course of rebuilding the hotel for the purpose of expansion, Müther's hall roof was unfortunately destroyed in 2002.

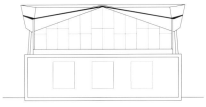

Bus Stop Waiting Room

Construction hypar shell, 7 x 7 m, shell thickness 5.5 cm, experimental shell for multi-purpose space in Rostock Lütten-Klein, identical in construction with the bus stop waiting rooms in Templin and Dranske (demolished) Use former bus stop waiting room Status well preserved, built-in units demolished, under historic protection Address Proraer Chaussee/Dollahner Straße, 18609 Ostseebad Binz

1967   Originally conceived as an experimental shell for the multi-purpose space in Rostock Lütten-Klein (see page 76), this hypar shell served for nearly twenty years as a bus waiting room. Temporary built-in units made the wait in wind and rain more comfortable. At the beginning of the 1990s, the built-in units were removed and since the redesign of the plaza in 2008, the since then free standing shell which stands by itself next to a traffic circle has been absolved of any function. The architect Harry Neumann (*1934), who worked in Ulrich Müther's office, collaborated on the design. Hypar shells identical in construction were also realized in 1969 for a bus stop waiting room in Templin and Dranske (1970). The geometric form of the hyperbolic paraboloid can be demonstrated exemplarily in the sculptural shell: The double curved, non-developable surface can be relatively easily cast into a formwork made of straight boards. Two groups of straight lines generate a surface, whose main curvatures run like a saddle in opposite directions. The Spanish engineer Félix Candela built many such concrete shells in Mexico. Drawing on the insights he gained from the Binz test shell, Müther designed several shell structures based on the hyperbolic paraboloid form used by Candela.

Lifeguard Rescue Tower 1

Construction two double curved shells assembled as a box, cantilever plate on a shaft, 5.5 x 5.5 m, shell thickness 7–16.5 cm Use life guard station Status demolished 1993 Address beach promenade, pier, 18609 Ostseebad Binz

1975 On July 28, 1912, the arrival point at the tip of the pier in Binz collapsed. More than one hundred people fell into the Baltic Sea, seventeen of whom drowned. On the one-year occasion of this terrible event, the Leipzig Deutsche Lebens-Rettungs-Gesellschaft (German Lifesaving Society) or DLRG, was founded. In 1975 Ulrich Müther received the commission to build the look-out and rescue tower for the lifeguards of the GDR's Red Cross on the location where the pier had formerly stood. The design by Dietrich Otto (*1943) who worked in Müther's office was presented at the Meister von Morgen convention (Master of Tomorrow convention, a science competition for youth). Both reinforced concrete shells for the look-out tower were cast in sand-molded forms. The halves were fitted together on location and mounted on the main support. The original design included a pole inside the shaft to speed the lifeguards' deployment, but in the course of the planning this was replaced by a cantilevering stairway. In 1993 the rescue tower was demolished and the Binz pier was rebuilt on its former location. A slightly different second lifeguard tower (see page 46), also built by Müther in 1981, is still standing on the southern beach promenade.

Lifeguard Rescue Tower 2

Construction two double curved shells assembled as a box, 5.5 x 5.5 m, shell thickness 3–5 cm Use until 2003 as lifeguard rescue tower Status renovated 2004 Address eastern beach promenade, beach stairway 6, 18609 Ostseebad Binz

1981 In 1979, Ulrich Müther began planning another lifeguard tower on the eastern beach promenade. He was able to make use of the first tower's form for the two shells of the new tower (see page 44). As before, the square masonry base, which was filled with sand for stability, was formed using wooden rib templates and was then covered with screed cement. This was in turn the basic form for the shell, in this case realized with even thinner walls. Müther was bolder this time: because he used a special ferrocement mixture, the normal amount of reinforcement could be greatly reduced and replaced with a few layers of hexagonal mesh (i.e. chicken wire). Gunite concrete also facilitated lighter and optically slimmer-looking shells. The tower was also reconceived to have a reduced profile in other ways: the shaft was shortened and the concrete cantilevering plate was eliminated. A simple steel stairway connects the observation room with the beach. The tower was taken out of service for lifeguard duty in 2003. Today, it is leased to Ms. Zydowitz-Müther for use as a gallery, exhibition space and lecture room. Since 2006, the branch office of the local registry office has also conducted wedding ceremonies in the gleaming white jewel set in the dunes of Binz.

Vacationers' Restaurant Szczecin

Construction two spaces, each comprising four umbrella shells, 11.25 x 11.25 m, on a square floor plan; two additional spaces, each with three umbrella shells, 10.2 x 7.2 m, on a rectangular floor plan, shell thickness 7 cm Collaboration with Robert Waterstraat of the Rostock housing combine Use restaurants, event rooms Status 1999 renovated, partially reconfigured Address Strandpromenade 74, 18609 Ostseebad Binz

1978   In 1956 the Freie Deutsche Gewerkschaftsbund (Free German Trade Union Federation, or FDGB) took over the Seeschloss to make it the first holiday retreat on the Binz beach promenade. Beginning in 1972, more vacation facilities were added. The Binz location was considered a showpiece of the FDGB until reunification. In 1988 alone, it was the destination for 144'000 vacationers. The employees of the former restaurant Szczecin had provided meals for the guests in the surrounding vacation homes since the late seventies. After the reunification, the restaurant complex was administered by a federal trust, until it was sold to the company IFA Hotels and Resorts in 1991. Today, the former restaurant is part of the IFA Ferienpark Rügen, where the four spaces are still used as restaurants and event spaces. The Rügen and Hiddensee rooms are enclosed by four free standing, square umbrella shells, connected by over-head lighting strips. In the course of the building's renovation in 1999, the form of the umbrella shells was concealed beneath a stepped cladding. The two smaller restaurants, Gryf and Vital are each enclosed by three asymmetric umbrella shells fitted together (see photo). Today the structure of the mobile and reusable scaffold is still recognizable on the underside of the shells.

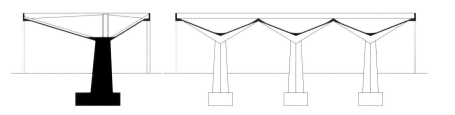

Swimming Pool Roof, Central Committee Clubhouse

Design asymmetrical suspended shell, 24.4 x 33.3 m, shell thickness 9 cm Collaboration with Kurt Tauscher from the Rostock housing combine Use indoor swimming pool Status well preserved, renovated Address Siedlung am Wald 22, 18586 Ostseebad Sellin

1977   The vacation hotel was built on the hill between Sellin and Baabe on behalf of Erich Honecker (1912–1994), who was at that time the general secretary of the central committee of the state party, the SED. The complex was completed in 1978 and was reserved for the middle level cadre of the party until it was privatized after German reunification. Today, the five star facility is known as the Cliff Hotel and offers its guests an extensive spa and wellness program including the swimming pool. Ulrich Müther determined the form of the suspended shell with the aid of a rubber skin, which he used for a test model. The stretched skin was stiffened with synthetic resin and then measured in order to process the shape digitally and calculate it. The full-size suspended membrane shell made of gunite on formwork is held in place at its edges by a secondary construction. It has the shape of an asymmetric funnel hanging freely from its edges. Its shape eliminates the need for a support at midpoint. The roof drains rainwater through the funnel, which originally terminated in a transparent downpipe made of plexiglass. In the course of its renovation, however, the roof was optically tied to the floor with a ring made of chrome steel, negating the impressive illusion that the roof was floating.

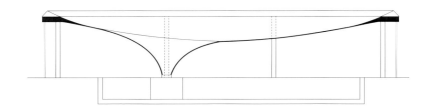

Restaurant Inselparadies (Island Paradise)

Construction umbrella shell made of four hypar surfaces, 17.6 x 17.6 m, shell thickness 8 cm
Use former restaurant Status deteriorating, under historic protection Address Fritz-
Reuter-Weg 21, 18586 Ostseebad Baabe

1966 The former restaurant on the beach promenade was a GDR showpiece and even in its current state of deterioration retains a touch of its old glamour. A kiosk for the beach guests was located on the ground floor, which is currently boarded up. This is also the location of the footing for the umbrella shell, consisting of four hypar surfaces joined together. A flight of stairs winds around the central support into the completely glass-enclosed upper floor, which offers a spectacular view of the beach and the Baltic Sea. The flush-mounted ceiling lamps of the formerly legendary Milch-Mocca-Bar, which was occasionally used as a discotheque, looked like a star filled night sky. The skeleton of the filigree steel window frames, as well as the concrete construction, is still intact. TLG Immobilien (the former Treuhand Liegenschaftsgesellschaft), which was founded in 1991 as a subsidiary of the Treuhandanstalt, itself dissolved in 1994, is the current owner of the property. The one storey utility annex on the upland side has already been demolished and the grounds behind the hypar shell, now under historic preservation, have been leveled, preparing the way for a potential buyer. To date, however, all renovation plans and reuse ideas put forth again and again by different potential investors have run aground.

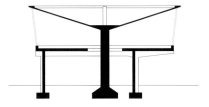

Book Kiosk

Construction funnel shell, diameter 8 m, shell thickness 5 cm Collaboration with Stefan Polónyi (statics) Use book kiosk Status well preserved, roof covered over, under historic protection Address Am Kurpark, 18586 Ostseebad Baabe

1971 A small, completely glass enclosed pavilion, whose roof emerges from a central, funnel shaped support stands in the spa gardens of the seaside resort of Baabe. During the summer it serves as a book kiosk and is home to an annex of the Inselbuchhandlung book shop from Bergen. As is the case with the bus stop waiting room in Binz, the book kiosk is an experimental building. In the framework of an event held by the International Association for Shell and Spatial Structures IASS, Ulrich Müther met the Hungarian professor Stefan Polónyi, who was working in West Germany. Müther created the book kiosk's funnel shell for him for research purposes. He erected a supporting scaffolding of 16 beams around a centrally located steel pipe. The concrete fabrication specialists surrounded the resulting support structure with hexagonal wire mesh (chicken wire) and sprayed several layers of concrete using the gunite technology. The circular construction served as a technological preliminary investigation for larger funnel shells. The form was eventually used for the large-scale construction of the ceramic museum Keramion in Frechen in North Rhine-Westphalia. That museum, designed by Peter Neufert (1925–1999), was built in collaboration with Polónyi immediately after the Baabe experiment in 1971.

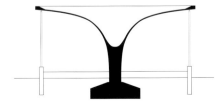

Refectory of E. Thälmann Pioneer Camp

Construction roof surface made of four hypar shells on a circumference of steel supports, 18 x 18 m, shell thickness 6 cm Use restaurant, to be converted into condominiums Status deteriorating, under renovation since 2002, under historic protection Address Am Strand, 18551 Borchtitz

1965 The district of Borchtitz in the township of Lietzow is located on federal highway 96 in the direction of Sagard. A narrow street branches off from the main road leading to the great Jasmund Bodden (lagoon), where the former Ernst Thälmann childrens' vacation camp is located. Müther used a design similar to that of the multi-purpose space in the House of the Steel Workers in Binz (see page 40) for the roof of the free standing dining hall. The pavilion, formerly completely glass enclosed, is on sandy ground just a few meters from the beach of the Great Jasmund Bodden and is surrounded by pines. Resting on a series of steel supports without touching the ground, the design of four conjoined hypar shells creates the illusion that the roof is floating. The corner columns are reinforced with diagonal struts. In 1972 additional buildings were built on the grounds of the pioneer camp (GDR boyscouts) in Borchtitz. Dietrich Otto, who was employed by Müther as an architect, designed four Finnish huts as bedrooms for the children in the immediate vicinity of the dining room. Müther executed them as test buildings for the folded roof shell construction he later realized in 1973 for the department store in Rostock Evershagen (see page 80). Unfortunately one of the huts was too near to the water and after a period of erosion, it fell into the water and could not be restored.

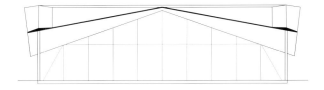

Swimming Pool Roof, Rügen Hotel

Construction shallow domed shell with circumferential beams, 20 x 20 m, shell thickness 10 cm Use indoor swimming pool Status well preserved, hotel renovated 1996 Address Seestraße 1, 18546 Sassnitz

1978 The Rügen Hotel was designed by the architect Herbert Sander (*1926) and built by a Swedish construction company in 1969. Owned by the Mitropa AG, which also operated the restaurants on the ferries from Sassnitz to Trelleborg, the hotel was reserved mostly for Swedish tourists until the end of the GDR regime. The large hotel restaurant is located in the low-rise building of the ensemble. Until the 1970s, the dining room overlooked the outdoor swimming pool and the Baltic Sea. Given regional climate factors and the ubiquitous flock of sea gulls circling overhead, the pool provided an extremely exposed and austere bathing experience. In order to address those inadequacies, Ulrich Müther received the commission in 1977 to plan and build a heated swimming pool with a roof in the place of the pre-existing pool. For the construction, Müther chose a gunite-built shallow domed shell with pre-stressed perimeter beams. The roof was covered in vegetation to have the appearance of a green hill across which the restaurant guests could look towards the Baltic Sea. In the course of the extensive renovation of the hotel in 1996, the swimming pool roof was for the most part maintained. Originally clad in cork granulate, the underside of the shell is currently clad with ornamental plastic acoustic tiles.

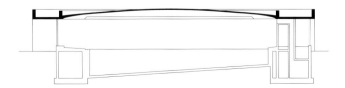

Music Pavilion Kurmuschel

Construction shell-shaped cantilever, gunite shells on wire mesh, radius 11 m, shell thickness 5–15 cm Collaboration with Dietmar Kuntzsch and Otto Patzelt Use music pavilion Status well preserved, renovated 2006 Address Kurplatz, 18546 Sassnitz

1987   The coast near the city of Sassnitz drops steeply to the water. The spa's main square with its expressively shaped music pavilion is located beneath a high, fortified wall at the eastern end of the beach promenade. The structure is known locally as the Kurmuschel or Concert Shell. The evocative form of the pavilion, which was completed in 1987, was designed by the architect Dietmar Kuntzsch (*1936). Ulrich Müther calculated and executed the shell construction in collaboration with the engineer Otto Patzelt (*1930). For the projecting roof composed of seven upwardly opening fan-like shells, a grid was first assembled from bent reinforcing rods, which were then covered with wire mesh. Gunite was then applied to the wire mesh. The shells and the two flanking storage rooms were sheathed in a white plaster. In addition to several regional firms, students from the College of Art in Berlin Weißensee were involved in the project. The inappropriately conventional looking trellis around the plaza today bears witness to the fact that the original plan for the grounds was never entirely realized. In the summer concerts and other cultural events are regularly held in the concert shell. The white-clad concrete form, laden with symbolism, is a jewel on the Sassnitz harbor promenade.

Restaurant Ostseeperle (Pearl of the Baltic)

Construction tilted hypar shell, 20 x 20 m, shell thickness 7 cm, identical in construction with the restaurants in Eberswalde and Hohenfelden Collaboration with Hans-Otto Möller Use former beach restaurant, vacant since 1990 Status conversion 2005–2009, under historic protection Address Hauptstraße 65, 18551 Glowe

1968   Not far from the spa's main plaza, at the eastern end of the village of Glowe, the Ostseeperle restaurant is located. The curved, tilted hypar shell is located directly behind a strip of sand dune, making it particularly eye-catching. Its fully glazed façade provides the former restaurant of the consumer cooperative society a spectacular view over the dunes to the Baltic Sea. In addition to the ground level restaurant seating, an upstairs gallery with additional seating is also contained within the building. The restaurant has space for up to 300 guests. Since 1990, the building has been vacant. In 2005 the private owner began the renovation for a new use which is complete today. The roof has been renovated, the glass façade replaced and in place of the utility block formerly attached on the side, a residency hotel is now located. A reopening of the Ostseeperle took place in 2009. Ulrich Müther was able to realize the building designed together with Hans-Otto Möller (1931–2004) that same year at other locations: Identical restaurants, each with a utility block adapted to the surroundings, are located at the dammed lake in Hohenfelden, Thuringia (see page 108), and in Eberswalde, Brandenburg (see page 107). Other similar buildings were carried out at slightly different scales.

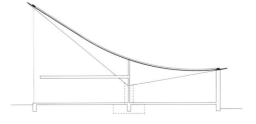

Open-Air Orchestra Pavilion

Construction hypar shell in wooden grid construction, 13 x 15.35 m, shell thickness 8 cm
Use formerly orchestra pavilion, today a storage shed Status very bad condition, defaced
Address Am Bodden 100, 18528 Ralswiek

1980 The famous Störtebeker Festspiele (festival) draws thousands of visitors in the summer from beyond Mecklenburg-Western Pomerania to the open-air stage on the banks of the Bodden lagoon. Since 1993, the former Rügenfestspiele (1959–1961 and 1980–1981) have been revived and now include costly sets. Meanwhile, behind the scenes, in an area off-limits to the public, the building that once served as the orchestra pavilion is still languishing. Built in 1980 as an elegant protective roof for the musicians of the Rügenfestspiele, it is a storage facility for the festivals' lighting equipment and is deteriorating rapidly. The double curved wooden grid construction, which is reminiscent of the structures of the West German engineer Frei Otto (*1925), is Müther's only shell construction realized in wood. The design was generated in just three months. For acoustic reasons, Ulrich Müther and his team decided in favor of a grid of wooden framing. Unfortunately today only a part of the great span is visible: an already badly damaged roofing felt installed in the 1990s covers the wooden construction, while a wall added at a later date disguises the original form from the front side. The ambitious structure is currently in an advanced state of decay.

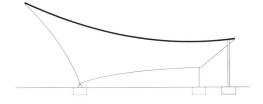

Bus Stop Waiting Room

Construction multiply curved gunite shell, ca. 4 x 5 m, height ca. 2.6 m Use bus stop waiting room Status well preserved Address Dorfstraße 19, 18528 Buschvitz

1974 The village of Buschvitz, about five kilometres north of Bergen, has approximately 230 inhabitants – and a curious bus stop. When a 1973 storm destroyed all the bus stop waiting rooms in the town, Ulrich Müther received a contract to design replacement structures. The design was by Dietrich Otto, one of the young architects working for him at the time who had received his degree in 1968 at the Technical University of Dresden (see elevation drawing of the preliminary design). After working for the Rostock housing combine for three years, Otto began working for Müther in 1971 in Binz. He also designed the rescue centers on the beach at Binz (see pages 44–47). For the assembly, Müther's employees assembled a scaffold made of bent reinforcing rods, wrapped them with hexagonal wire mesh which they then coated with gunite. This was then troweled and sanded by hand, which presented some difficulties because of the spherical form. The little building was originally intended as a prototype for a series of bus stop waiting rooms. Because of the manufacturing expense and the aesthetically mediocre result, no more were realized. The residents affectionately call the round structure the "diving helmet" because of its shape.

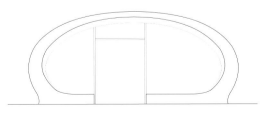

Student Restaurant

Construction six umbrella shells, each 12 x 12 m, shell thickness 6 cm Collaboration with Rostock housing combine Use student restaurant Status demolished 2002 Address Straße der DSF 5, 18528 Bergen-South

1974 The district of Bergen-South was created from the mid-sixties on and consists mainly of large residential housing in prefabricated slab construction. On the street of Deutsch-Sowjetische Freundschaft (DSF), the Rostock housing combine built a restaurant complex for the inhabitants of the new residential area. The students of the polytechnic and expanded secondary school were also served in the building. From the standpoint of use, the building was comparable to the one-storey restaurant complexes in Rostock Lütten-Klein, Stralsund or Magdeburg-North (see pages 78, 92, 109). However, its spatial division differed markedly from those: the rectangular floor plan of the two-storey complex corresponded exactly to the roof area of the six umbrella shells and was built without any additional annexes. Smaller restaurants, pubs and side rooms were located on the ground floor, while in the upper storey, a large dining hall was enclosed by one of Müther's hypar shell roofs. The building was used for a few years after German reunification but the various merchants did not enjoy any great success there. Consequently, its owner, TLG Immobilien decided in favor of demolition in 2002. Today, a housing facility for senior citizens is located on the site of the former restaurant complex.

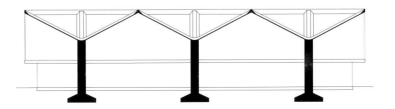

Gymnasium

Construction two double curved shallow domed shells on concrete columns, 15 x 15 m, shell thickness 8 cm Use school gymnasium Status well preserved, roof unrenovated Address Hermann-Matern-Straße 1, 18569 Gingst

1985 In the west on the island of Rügen, about 15 kilometers from Bergen, is the township of Gingst. Its school was built in 1971, and a gymnasium was supposed to be added to it soon after. Only in 1983, on behalf of the adult education division of the Rügen district council, did Ulrich Müther begin planning a site-neutral prototype for a series of school gymnasiums. In deference to the "local exigencies" in Gingst, the project included a one storey wing at the side of the standard gymnasium to accommodate dressing rooms and bathrooms. Under the direction of the assistant director Frank Siepelt (*1953) of the VEB Spezialbetonbau Rügen, the architect Harry Neumann (*1934) was entrusted with the project management. The gym roof, consisting of two shallow domed shells is held all around by a pre-stressed edge girder resting on regularly positioned concrete columns. In order to improve the gym's acoustics, wood fiber-integrated cement boards were laid on the formwork before spraying on the concrete. Their texture is still visible on the ceiling's underside today. Because of the expense and labor intensity, however, Müther's prototype did not prove to be feasible for serial construction. The gymnasium remained a one-off experiment and other types were later developed for schools.

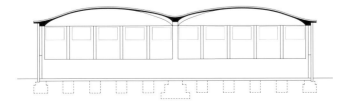

Hanseatic City of Rostock

Convention Center

Construction two juxtaposed hypar shells, each 20 x 20 m, shell thickness 7 cm Collaboration with Erich Kaufmann and Günther Ackermann (statics) Use former convention center, today an auto dealership with repair shop Status well preserved, under historic protection Address Libellenweg 3, 18069 Rostock Schutow

1966   In just 150 days, Ulrich Müther and his employees from the Produktionsgenossenschaft des Handwerks (PGH) Bau Binz planned and completed the hypar shells for the convention center intended for the Ostseemesse (Baltic Sea Fair) construction and mineral oil exposition in Rostock. The fair, with its extensive selection of goods, was considered a symbol for the increasing economic prosperity of the GDR. The bustle surrounding the exhibition offered a welcome distraction, especially in the 1960s. The opening celebration of the fair in front of Kaufmann and Müther's building represented an opportunity to demonstrate the shell construction method to the greater public as well as to the party leadership for the first time. Because of their symbolic content, the two juxtaposed hypar shells tapped the pulse of the age. Their expressively jutting roofs embodied the self-image of the emerging State. There was therefore a strong response to Müther's shells, and during the fair, he was able to make important contacts which led to more commissions. The Handelsorganisation (State Trade Organization) took notice of the young engineer from Binz: The restaurant Inselparadies in Baabe (see page 52) was built on its commission that same year, followed two years later by the Teepott in Warnemünde (see page 88).

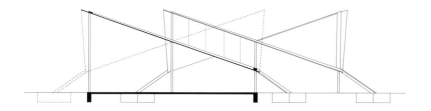

Multi-Purpose Hall

Construction four conjoined hypar shells, 47.3 x 47.3 m, shell thickness 7 cm Collaboration with Erich Kaufmann, Carl-Heinz Pastor and Hans Fleischhauer from the Rostock housing combine Use former multi-purpose hall, today retail and service center Status well preserved, renovated 2004, under historic protection Address Warnowallee 25, 18107 Rostock Lütten-Klein

1968   Lütten-Klein, the largest housing area in Rostock for about 36'000 inhabitants was built between 1965 und 1975 along the Warnowallee. The multi-purpose space with department store, fish shops, restaurant, bar and grill and two large public spaces was built as the so-called main center for the new housing area. The ground floor consists in part of non-bearing brick walls, while the upper glazed area features a striking façade of aluminum sun-shade louvers. Three of the four hyperbolic paraboloid shells which comprise the roof were manufactured from ready-mixed concrete. For the construction of the fourth shell, Müther was able for the first time to use his new gunite device, which he had procured from West Germany for the fourth shell. In order to check the accuracy of his force calculations, Müther carried out measurements with an experimental shell in Binz beforehand (see page 42). Pre-stressed tie rods beneath the floor level absorb the horizontal forces of the shells, which are carried by the support struts. Constantly changing uses and the lack of maintenance led in the 1990s to a situation in which the demolition of the hall was often discussed. Following renovation, the building was finally designated for use as a retail and service center.

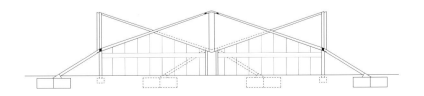

Restaurant Complexes Szczecin and Riga

Construction six umbrella shells, 12 x 12 m, shell thickness 6 cm, identical in construction with restaurants in Stralsund Knieper-West and Magdeburg-Nord Collaboration with Hans-Christian Brümmer from the Rostock housing combine Use former restaurants, Riga is today a retail center Status Szczecin: deteriorating, vacant; Riga: renovated Address Szczecin: Kopenhagener Straße 1, Riga: Turkuer Straße 57, 18107 Rostock Lütten-Klein

1973 The Szczecin and Riga restaurant complexes were built at the same time and are for the most part identical in construction. Their centrally located spaces are characterized by Müther's umbrella shell constructions, surrounded on three sides by one-storey low-rises. Because of the multiple uses they served, such as student cafeteria, restaurant, club and bar, beer pub and childrens' library, the complexes were local centers for the new housing area. The multi-purpose restaurant Baltic (Warnowallee 20a), whose eight umbrella shells were also realized by Müther at about the same time, is located nearby. Hans-Christian Brümmer (*1937) of the Rostock housing combine designed the buildings. The German artist Heinz Wodzicka (*1930) was commissioned for the interior design. After German reunification, the wall murals were painted over by the new owners. The restaurant Szczecin has been vacant for several years and is deteriorating (see photo). There is currently a plan to tear down the building and replace it with a building for assisted living. Also in the former restaurant Riga, it has been quite some time since one could enjoy one's meal in the midst of socialist wall murals: since the renovation in the 1990s, the spaces have been used for a retail center.

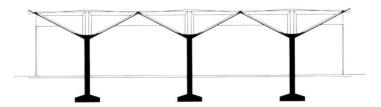

Department Store

Construction folded roof in three fields, 57 x 42.4 m, shell thickness 10 cm Collaboration with Peter Baumbach and Dieter Jastram from the Rostock housing combine Use former department store, today service and retail center Status well preserved, conversion 2005, expansion and ceiling installation Address Bertolt-Brecht-Straße 23, 18106 Rostock Evershagen

1973   Evershagen was the second housing area to be created between 1969 and 1974 after Lütten-Klein in the northwest of Rostock. The architects Peter Baumbach (*1940) and Dieter Jastram (*1930) from the Rostock housing combine developed the construction type of the department store building. At the beginning of the 1970s, the planners of the combine were so busy that a team of Danzig architects was entrusted with the implementation planning. Ulrich Müther was asked to do the design and realization of the centrally-located folded roof shell construction for the so-called Local Supply Center. From the standpoint of statics, folded roof shells, like other shell types, belong to the group of spatial surface-supported structures. In addition to the department store, the building also contained a multi-purpose space with terrace, a restaurant and an administration area. The same design was realized again a little while later as an identical project reusing the same design in the nearby district of Schmarl (Kolumbusring 61). The current owner TLG Immobilien renovated the Evershagen building complex and department store in 2005 for use as a service and retail center. Unfortunately, since the renovation the suspended ceiling panels block the view from below of the folded roof construction on the inside.

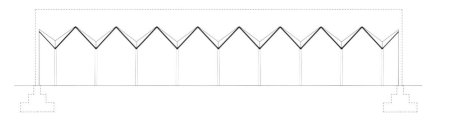

Restaurant Kosmos

Construction three hypar shells, each 20 x 20 m, shell thickness 6.3 cm Collaboration with Wolfgang Reinhard, Robert Waterstraat and Kurt Tauscher from the Rostock housing combine, interior design by Fritz Hering Use former restaurant, today retail and service center Status totally renovated and reshaped 1991, renovated 2008 Address Nobelstraße 50, 18059 Rostock Südstadt

1970 One of the first large scale housing projects for 20'000 inhabitants was realized with Rostock's Südstadt district between 1961 and 1965. Built using a large prefabricated panelized construction method, the buildings became popularly referred to as "Plattenbauten", or pre-fabs. Today, 13'000 inhabitants still live in the district. Since 2003, a streetcar line has connected the district with the Rostock center. Located in a striking setting on the city's south ring, the former Restaurant Kosmos and the department store Südstadt-Center, built in 1993, form a central reference point. Since its opening, Kosmos functioned architecturally and socially as a showpiece of the GDR State. The building lost its original charm after the renovations in 1991 and 2008, when the original rounded volumes under the shells (see section view) were removed. Four side annexes positioned between the hypar shells weakly imitate their expressively projecting gables. Today, because of the introduction of many subdivisions and unrelated functions, the interior space's large-scale spatial effect has been lost. In addition, snack stands and the streetcar infrastructure block the formerly spectacular view of the imposing supporting structure from the south ring road. All that remains is the view of Ulrich Müther's Kosmos from the upper storeys of the surrounding pre-fabs.

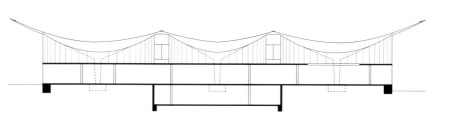

Catholic Church

Construction hypar shell, 23 x 23 m, shell thickness 7 cm Collaboration with Gisbert Wolf, Rudolf Lasch and Kurt Tauscher from the Rostock housing combine Use church Status well preserved, roof sealing replaced, under historic protection Address Häktweg 4–6, 18057 Rostock Center

1971 In 1969, the Rostock city council assembly decided on an extensive restructuring of the city center, which included the Rostock Christuskirche (Church of Christ). Despite numerous protests from the city's citizens, it was demolished in August, 1971. Following a feasibility study and design proposal by the Schwerin architect Gisbert Wolf (*1937), the director of the Rostock building agency of the Evangelical-Lutheran Church, a new Catholic parish center was built on the edge of the inner city, pushing the Catholic denomination, seen by the State as undesirable, to the periphery. In collaboration with the municipal architect Dr. Rudolf Lasch (1930–1993) and the Rostock housing combine in the person of Kurt Tauscher (1922–1984), Ulrich Müther developed the hypar shell for the roof of the new church space. The roof area was constructed as a steel framework and manufactured with gunite technology. Its horizontal forces were distributed along the walls of the confessionals on the sides. As with many hypar shells, both of the side plinths are connected beneath the floor with pre-stressed tie rods, but in contrast to most of Müther's shell constructions, the building is less elegant because of the plinths. In 2003, a technical study resulted in a favorable status report.

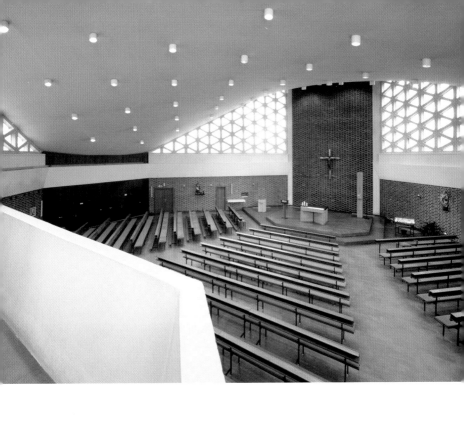

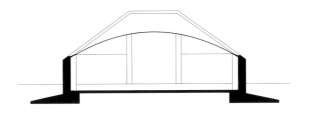

Company Restaurant ITV

Construction four umbrella shells, each 10.8 x 10.8 m, shell thickness 6 cm Collaboration with Otto Dabel (statics) Use former company restaurant Status deteriorating, vacant Address Dierkower Damm 39, 18146 Rostock Center

1975 Somewhat removed from Rostock's city center on the eastern end of the city harbor, is the former headquarters of the engineering, civic and road construction combine. The different strands of this influential organization, which had subsidiaries in many cities, were brought together here. Ulrich Müther planned and realized a striking variation of his usually linearly adjacent or consecutively positioned umbrella shells for the construction of the company restaurant: four windmill-like umbrella shells grouped around a central skylight span the space. The rhythmic façade development from street to courtyard distinguishes the otherwise sober building. The undersides of each of the four umbrellas formed by hypar surfaces are painted white and the pronounced impression left by the formwork provides a contrast to the filigree wood cladding of the service area, which protrudes into the utility rooms located on two sides. A low parapet subdivides the non-load bearing glass façade, which permits a lot of sunlight to suffuse the dining room, but now only sheds light on the increasingly deteriorating state of the space. Disused since the 1990s, the building is not under historic protection and belongs to a private real estate company. It is likely that the now badly damaged property will be demolished.

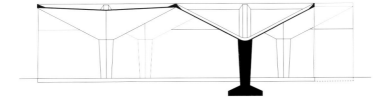

Restaurant Teepott (Teapot)

Construction shell construction consisting of three hypar shells, radius 20 m, shell thickness 7 cm Collaboration with Erich Kaufmann, Carl-Heinz Pastor and Hans Fleischhauer from the Rostock housing combine Use restaurants, shops, offices, museum Status renovated 2002, under historic protection Address Seepromenade 1, 18119 Warnemünde

1968 This striking building's name has a long history. Already in 1927, Walter Butzek (1886–1965) built a circular tea pavilion with a domed metal roof called the Teepott. Because the original burned down in 1945, the GDR trade organization decided to plan a new restaurant at the same location in 1966. Under the direction of Erich Kaufmann, the architect in chief of the housing combine, Müther created a new trademark for Warnemünde with his signal roof construction consisting of three hypar shells. The building became vacant in 1991 and demolition was under discussion. After extensive renovation, the Teepott reopened in 2002 with several restaurants and shops. The new uses fortunately saved the building from demolition. In the framework of the renovation, the metal sculpture by the artist Fritz Kühn (1910–1967), which previously surrounded the building, was removed and put in storage. To accommodate small shops and restaurants, the renovation architects have compartmentalized the expansive space beneath the shell roof of the restaurant which formerly occupied the entire upper storey. Müther, who had intervened heavily on behalf of retaining the shell construction, laconically commented that the light partition walls could at least easily be removed.

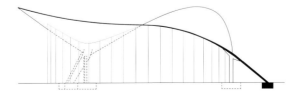

Stralsund Wismar Schwerin Neubrandenburg

Restaurant Complex City of Stralsund

Construction six umbrella shells, each 12 x 12 m, shell thickness 6 cm, identical in construction to restaurants in Rostock Lütten-Klein and Magdeburg-Nord Use former restaurants, today different shops, dance sport club, restaurants Status well preserved, from 1991–1995 subdivided and altered Address Maxim-Gorki-Straße 32, 18435 Stralsund Knieper-West

1975 The Hanseatic city of Stralsund currently has just under 60'000 inhabitants. The old medieval city has belonged since 2002 to the UNESCO World Heritage and with its gothic brick buildings and typical Hanseatic city fabric, the city has become a tourist attraction. On a short visit to the city, most travelers overlook the outlying city districts, which were built in the 1960s and 70s. The restaurant complex city of Stralsund is located in Knieper-West, the largest development area of the city, built beginning in 1964 according to the designs of the architects Karl-Heinz Wegner (1928–2007) and Siegfried Mecklenburg (*1932). Müther had already realized this building type in 1973 in Rostock Lütten-Klein (see page 78). The Stralsund variation can best be described as a reused design project. Until 1991, the building accommodated a cafeteria for students, a library and several pubs in the low structures on three sides of the building. As a result of various alterations, the large hall with its umbrella shells was subdivided several times to house various functions and rented out by the property management of the city of Stralsund. Today a video library, dance sport club and a carpet store (see photo) share the space beneath Müther's umbrellas, now perceptible only in fragments.

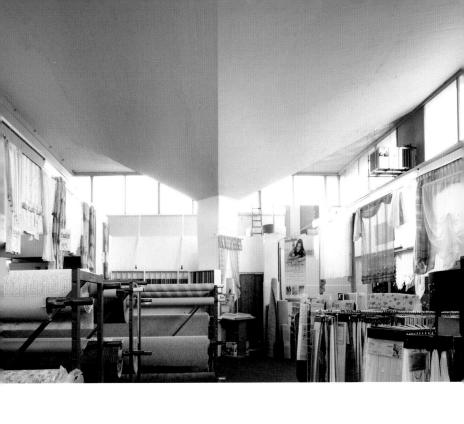

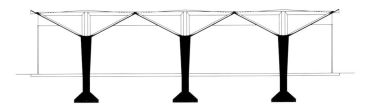

Multi-Purpose Space for Church Community Center

Construction two conjoined hypar shells on a marginal pillar, 11.4 x 11.4 m, shell thickness 6 cm Collaboration with Günter Kirmes Use multi-purpose and church space Status well preserved Address Lindenstraße 151, 18435 Stralsund Knieper-West

1977 In the mid 1970s, the Stralsund housing district of Knieper-West had more than 10'000 inhabitants. There were many younger families and 25 percent of the population was Protestant. Even as the construction of the new district began in the late 1960s, the clamor for a church was unmistakable. Politically undesired by the atheist regime, a new church building was considered possible only on the boundary of the district. In 1975, the Evangelical parish of St. Nikolai received the long-sought construction permit for their outpost. The parish center was financed by a special program, paid for by West German churches, which had originally been reserved for historic buildings. Looking for a contemporary interpretation for this building program, the church's high council engaged Ulrich Müther, who in turn had the architect Dietrich Otto develop the concept for the primary design. The two double curved hypar surfaces of the roof correspond to a halved umbrella shell like those often used by Müther. The artist Christof Grüger (*1926) received the contract for the design of the concrete glass window. In 1977, the Evangelical parish opened the externally unpretentious ensemble of church space, youth house, event and community room, with two apartments and a belfry.

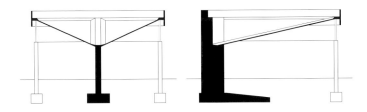

Engineering College Cafeteria

Construction four umbrella shells, each 14.4 x 12.4 m; two umbrella shells, each 14.4 x 12.8 m; one umbrella shell 12.8 x 12.8 m, shell thickness 6 cm Collaboration with Arno Claus Martin, Siegfried Fischer and the VEB Ingenieurhochbaukombinat (Structural Engineering Combine) Rostock Use former canteen complex, today it houses a discotheque in the basement Status well preserved, partially vacant since 2003 Address Bürgermeister-Haupt-Straße 1, 23966 Wismar

1975 The Wismar-Südwest district was built in the 1970s around existing buildings. In the same decade, the Engineering College cafeteria was also built, and was foreseen as a community center for the new district of the city. Ulrich Müther's umbrella shells span the two large dining rooms and a smaller refreshments room, providing a design accent for an otherwise sober building. In the 1990s, the campus was extended to the northwest, so that the cafeteria was no longer on the campus. Since the facility was in need of renovation at any rate, the college decided to give up the property. The cafeteria ceased operations in 2003 and since then, large areas of the former catering complexes are no longer used. The improvised interior renovations complete since then by a discotheque operator who has rented the basement disguise the original use. Despite the completely haphazard transfigurations, the structure of the original building is well preserved and it would not be too late to use the spaces again in the future. It is only logical, from the perspective of today that an engineering college would hardly want to abandon the building that was realized in Müther's hypar shell constructions.

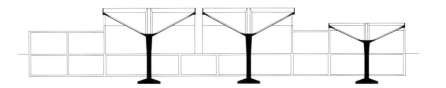

Restaurant Panorama

Construction hypar shell, 20 x 20 m, shell thickness 6.3 cm Collaboration with Georg Schneider and the VEB Hauptinvestor Komplexer Wohnungsbau (main investor residential building) Use restaurant, today also as apartment Status well preserved, conversion 1993, with various installations Address Johannes-Brahms-Straße 65, 19059 Schwerin

1972 The former trade fair restaurant Panorama is located in the Weststadt district, in the immediate vicinity of the Schwerin sport and convention center built from 1958 to 1962. Located on a natural ridge on the grounds above Wittenburger Straße, it was commissioned as an extension of the gastronomic services for large events by the VEB Hauptinvestor Komplexer Wohnungsbau. The architect Georg Schneider and Ulrich Müther designed the two storey building together with the building owner. The multi-purpose hall and restaurant Achteck (Octagon) (1971) opposite it was built at the same time. In the 1980s, it featured a disco that became known far beyond the borders of Schwerin. After German reunification, the restaurant Panorama was vacant for a time until the operator of a Chinese restaurant took the risk to reopen it after it was renovated. The ground floor, on which the lobby, ancillary rooms and a central dance floor were located, was changed drastically. The apartment of the proprietors is now located next to the entrance and the large hospitality space on the upper floor under the shell roof was subdivided several times. Nonetheless, the observation deck on the south side was left unchanged and continues to provide restaurant guests with a spot to tarry.

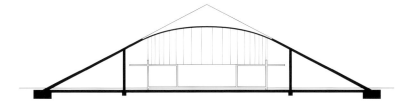

Municipal Hall

Construction four tilted hypar shells fitted together, each 20 x 20 m, total surface area 42 x 42 m, shell thickness 7 cm Collaboration with Karl Kraus and Kurt Ihloff (statics) Use multi-purpose space Status well preserved, roof renovated, various annexes, under historic protect-ion Address Parkstraße 2, 17033 Neubrandenburg

1969 The structural work for the shells of the Municipal Hall in Neubrandenburg was completed in just seven months. The building was completed for the 20th anniversary of the GDR in October 1969. In accordance with the practice at the time, the construction work began simultaneously with the planning. Starting from the basic module of the hypar shell that had been conceived shortly before for the Ostseeperle restaurant in Glowe (see page 62), Ulrich Müther and the architect Karl Kraus developed the design for the municipal hall. The influ-ence of Félix Candela's much more expressive church of San José Obrero in Monterrey from 1960 cannot be overlooked (see page 28). Four identical shells on top of a square floor plan are connected by a strip of skylights. They meet at the highest point above the middle of the hall in a crown-like cap. The footings for the inclined compression struts of the roof surfaces are con-nected with prestressed tie rods under the floor of the main space. All ancillary rooms are located in the four one-storey annexes at the building's corners; their roofs are also comprised of flat hyperbolic-paraboloid surfaces realized in gunite. Along with other broadcasts, the popular GDR entertainment pro-gram "Schlagerstudio" (Hit Studio) was recorded in the primary space. The Municipal Hall is still used today for events.

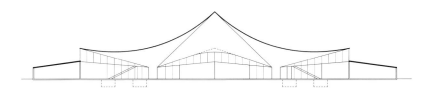

Catholic Church St. Josef and Lukas

Construction two hypar shells, 23.5 x 30 m and 17.6 x 23 m, shell thickness each 7 cm Collaboration with Erhard Russow, interior design by Harald Heyde Use church with service rooms Status well preserved, roof renovated, under historic protection Address Heidmühlenstraße 9, 17033 Neubrandenburg

1980   When the existing Catholic Church in Neubrandenburg had to make way for road construction in the 1970s, the parish council applied to the city council for a permit to construct a new building. In the framework of a special construction program, the funds needed were gathered in 1975 and excavation work began in December 1976. The new building was opened in 1980 and combines a space for worship, rooms for the community, youth activity, teaching and music, and an apartment for the chaplain. Although the preliminary design by Müther's architect Dietrich Otto envisioned an almost completely enclosed brick façade, the architect entrusted with the execution, Erhard Russow (*1933), developed a bulkhead-like articulated mantle. Its vertical window bands distinguish the exterior façade as well as the church interior. The hypar shell roofs were built using gunite. As was the case with the church construction in Rostock (see page 84), the compression struts outside were omitted here. The forces are distributed over vertical supports, which are tied together beneath the floor with tie rods. In order to compensate the asymmetrical support of the larger shell, the protruding corner of the shorter roof section is counterweighted by hidden concrete weights.

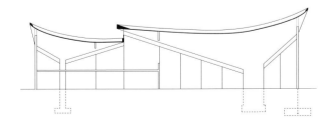

Appendix

Shell Structures in Germany and worldwide

Index

Templin 1, 5, 16

Eberswalde 2

24 Osnabrück   Wolfsburg 21   Berlin 10, 14, 25
                                Potsdam 20
        28 Hanover

                                            Cottbus 17
            Magdeburg 7, 11, 15, 18, 19

        Ermsleben 6
        Hettstedt 18   27 Leipzig
            Halle 3   4 Lonnevitz
                        Döbeln 9
        Hohenfelden 8   22 Jena   Dresden 13
Fulda 26   Altenberg 23
                    12 Oberhof

1 Cultural Center Bürgergarten

Hypar shell, 20.5 x 20.5 m, shell thickness 7 cm, with Horst Mallek, deteriorated, Templin, Brandenburg, 1967

2 Restaurant in the Tierpark (Zoo)

Tilted hypar shell, 20 x 20 m, shell thickness 7 cm, identical in construction with restaurants in Glowe, Halle and Hohenfelden, renovated, Eberswalde, Brandenburg, 1968

3 Restaurant on the Heinrich-Heine-Felsen (rock)

tilted hypar shell, 20 x 20 m, shell thickness 7 cm, with F. Hübner, identical in construction with restaurants in Eberswalde, Glowe and Hohenfelden, demolished, Halle, Saxony-Anhalt, 1968

4 Motorway Restaurant

Hypar shell, 16 x 16 m, shell thickness 5.8 cm, with Ingo Schönrock Architects Collective, demolished, Lonnevitz (District of Oschatz), Saxony, 1968

5 Bus Stop Waiting Room

Hypar shell, 7 x 7 m, shell thickness 5.5 cm, with Horst Mallek, identical in construction with bus stop waiting rooms in Binz and Dranske, renovated, Templin, Brandenburg, 1969

6 Company Restaurant PGH Tonfunk

Hypar shell, 18 x 18 m, shell thickness 6.6 cm, with Ingo Schönrock Architects Collective, identical in construction with the restaurant in Döbeln, demolished 2003, Anger 20, Ermsleben, Saxony-Anhalt, 1969

7 Exhibition Center in the Rotehorn Cultural Park
Four conjoined hypar shells, each 24 x 24 m, with a total of 48 x 48 m, shell thickness 7 cm, with Horst Freytag and Günther Ackermann (statics), unrenovated, Heinrich-Heine-Platz 1, Magdeburg, Saxony-Anhalt, 1970

8 Beach Restaurant on a dammed lake
Tilted hypar shell, 20 x 20 m, shell thickness 7 cm, identical in construction with the restaurants in Eberswalde, Glowe and Halle, preserved, Erfurter Straße, Hohenfelden, Thüringen, 1970

9 Park Restaurant Bürgergarten
Hypar shell, 18 x 18 m, shell thickness 6.6 cm, with Ingo Schönrock Architects Collective, identical in construction with the restaurant in Ermsleben, demolished 1995, Döbeln, Saxony, 1970

10 Television Tower Pedestrian Base
Folded roof shell construction, measuring 36 x 75 m in total, sole execution by Ulrich Müther, with Walter Herzog and Heinz Aust, well preserved, Panoramastraße 1, Berlin, 1971

11 Large Scale Sculpture
Free, double curved shell, 12 m high, shotcreted without formwork, sole execution by Ulrich Müther, with Horst Freytag, well preserved, Elbuferpromenade, Magdeburg, Saxony-Anhalt, 1972

12 Luge and Bobsled Run
Free shell construction, 1033 m long, wet spray technique, shotcreted without a shell, with W. Möbius and U. Gurgel, renovated 1987, well preserved, Jägerstraße 10, Oberhof, Thüringen, 1972

13 Rowing Center Blasewitz
Four conjoined hypar shells, each 18 x 18 m, with a total of 36 x 36 m, umbrella shell, 13.5 x 13.5 m, shell thickness 6 cm, with Ingo Schönrock Architects Collective, renovated 2005, Oehmestraße 2, Dresden, Saxony, 1972

14 Large Restaurant Ahornblatt (Maple Leaf)
Five attached hypar shell segments, each 22 x 35 m, shell thickness 7 cm, with Gerhard Lehmann, Rüdiger Plaethe, Helmut Stingl, demolished 2000, Gertrudenstraße/Fischerinsel 12, Berlin, 1973

15 Shop Projection for the distribution firm RFT
Four umbrella shells, 12 x 12 m, shell thickness 6 cm, with Horst Freytag, unrenovated, Julius-Bremer-Straße/Max-Otten-Straße, Magdeburg, Saxony-Anhalt, 1973

16 Repair and Motor Transport Hall
Ten umbrella shells, each 12 x 12 m, shell thickness 6 cm, with Horst Mallek, renovated, Templin, Brandenburg, 1973

17 Yuri Gagarin Space Flight Planetarium
Spherical shell, diameter 12.5 m, network of rods shotcreted, with Carl Zeiss Jena, Lindenplatz 21, Cottbus, Brandenburg, 1974

18 Restaurant
Six umbrella shells, each 12 x 12 m, shell thickness 6 cm, identical in construction with the restaurant complexes Riga and Szczecin in Rostock Lütten-Klein and Stralsund Knieper-West, Magdeburg-Nord, Saxony-Anhalt, 1975

19 Restaurant Kosmos
Nine umbrella shells, each 12 x 12 m, shell thickness 6 cm, with Horst Freytag, well preserved, Otto-Baer-Straße 8, Magdeburg-Reform, Saxony-Anhalt, 1975

20 Shore Pavilion Seerose (Water Lily)
Eight-part rosette made of hypar segments, diameter 23 m, shell thickness 7 cm, with Dieter Ahting, well preserved, Breite Straße 24, Potsdam, Brandenburg, 1983

21 Space Flight Planetarium Spacemaster
Spherical shell, diameter 17.8 m, shell thickness 9–15 cm, shotcreted network of rods, with Volker Kersten, Erich Martinoff, Hans Struhk, Gertrud Schille and Carl Zeiss Jena, well preserved, Uhlandweg 2, Wolfsburg, Lower Saxony, 1983

22 Large Planetarium of the Ernst Abbe Foundation
Spherical shell, diameter 23.5 m, shell thickness 10 cm, shotcreted network of rods, with Antje Dombrowski and Carl Zeiss Jena, demolished and replaced 1996 with a new construction, Jena, Thuringia, 1985

23 Luge and Bobsled Course
Free, double curved shell, 1413 m long, shotcreted without formwork, with Udo Gurgel, well preserved, Neuer Kohlgrundweg 1, Altenberg, Saxony, 1986

24 Planetarium in the Museum am Schölerberg
Inner dome, steel network of rods, suspended Rabitz plaster projection dome, diameter 8 m, with Carl Zeiss Jena, well preserved, Am Schölerberg 8, Osnabrück, Lower Saxony, 1986

25 Zeiss Large Planetarium in the Thälmann-Park

Spherical shell, external diameter 30 m, internal diameter 23 m, shell thickness 12–15 cm, shotcreted network of rods, with Gottfried Hein, Hubert Schlotter, Carl Zeiss Jena, well preserved, Prenzlauer Allee 80, Berlin, Brandenburg, 1987

26 Zeiss Small Planetarium

Inner dome, steel network of rods, suspended Rabitz plaster projection dome, diameter 6 m, with Carl Zeiss Jena, well preserved, Vonderau-Museum, Jesuitenplatz 2, Fulda, Hesse, 1989

27 Planetarium in the Zoological Garden

Inner dome, steel network of rods, suspended aluminium projection dome, diameter 8 m, shotcreted network of rods, with Carl Zeiss Jena, closed in 1995, Pfaffendorfer Straße 29, Leipzig, Saxony, 1992

28 Michael Church

Hypar shell construction, static calculation by Büro GRBV Hanover, sole execution by Ulrich Müther, Ellernstraße 44, Hanover, Lower Saxony, 1992

1 Space Flight Planetarium Spacemaster
Spherical shell, five attached hypar shell segments, internal diameter 15 m, total area 60 x 58 m, shell thickness 7 cm, shotcreted network of rods, with Gertrud Schille, Carl Zeiss Jena, Georg Zumpe, Al Fath Street, Tripoli, Libya, 1981

2 Space Flight Planetarium Spacemaster
Internal dome, steel network of rods, suspended aluminum projection surface, diameter 15.5 m, destroyed in 1990, National Museum, Safat, Al-Kuwait, Kuwait, 1985

3 Planetarium in the Heureka Science Center
Inner dome, steel network of rods, suspended aluminium projection surface, diameter 17.5 m, with Jan Müller, Mikko Heikkinen and Markku Komonen, well preserved, Tiedepuisto 1, Tikkurila, Vantaa, Finland, 1989

In addition to shell constructions, Ulrich Müther built a large number of conventional buildings in the course of his professional career, which were not documented in this volume. The various speed skating and cycling tracks built in Germany and abroad were also not included. In contrast with the free-standing shell constructions in this publication, their double curved gunite surfaces rest completely on the ground.

The first large-scale planetarium in the world was the Zeiss-Planetarium built in Jena in 1926 by Carl Zeiss Jena. In addition to the domed shell built for the Schott glass works Jena in 1924, it is considered one of the first modern shell constructions made of reinforced concrete. Since then the Jena firm built an impressive number of planetariums of different sizes in Germany and worldwide.

The collaboration between Ulrich Müther and Carl Zeiss Jena began in 1972 with the planning of a small planetarium in Cottbus, which was completed two years later. In the 1980s in the framework of this cooperation, a series of planetarium buildings were built in Germany and abroad for which Ulrich Müther was in most cases responsible. Some of the domes were executed as spherical shells made of gunite, while others were built as three-dimensional steel rod networks with suspended projection surfaces made of aluminum plates or Rabitz plaster light-weight domes. The index assembled here contains all the work completed for Carl Zeiss Jena planetariums. There are additional, in some cases publicly announced projects for planetariums and mosques which were never realized.

All dates of completion refer to the year of opening. In most cases the structural work – and thereby Ulrich Müther's shell construction – was completed several months beforehand. However, there can also be an interval of several years between completion of structural work and final completion.

When possible, the architects involved in the design and the execution are mentioned, as well as the engineers responsible for the structural analysis. The information about the buildings outside Mecklenburg-Western Pomerania reflects the current research status of the Müther-Archive of the College of Wismar and the research of the authors. There is no definitive catalogue of all Ulrich Müther buildings at present. The processing of the archive materials concerning the work of Ulrich Müther is ongoing and will take several years. Suggestions, corrections and augmentations are welcome. Contact address: info@ulrichmuether.com

Bibliography
Ulrich Müther

Many of the shell constructions by Ulrich Müther were publicized at the time they were built in the official architecture magazine of the GDR *Deutsche Architektur* (1957–1974) and *Architektur der DDR* (1974–1990). By the 1990s, his buildings were for the most part forgotten and resurfaced again in the German media only in 2000. Therefore, in order to illustrate the history of their reception, the bibliography is chronologically organized.

Monographs
Susanne Burmester (ed.), *Müther*, Putbus: Kunstverein Rügen e. V., 2008
Wilfried Dechau (ed.), *Kühne Solitäre. Ulrich Müther – Schalenbaumeister der DDR*, Stuttgart: Deutsche Verlagsanstalt, 2000.

Essays
Klaus Stiglat, "Ulrich Müther", in: Klaus Stiglat (ed.), *Bauingenieure und ihr Werk*, Berlin: Ernst & Sohn, 2004, pp. 258–262.
Oliver Herwig, "Escaping from Slab Construction. Ulrich Müther's Shell Artworks", in: Oliver Herwig (ed.), *Featherweights. Light, Mobile and Floating Architecture*, Munich: Prestel, 2003, pp. 56–65.
Wilfried Dechau, "Ulrich Müther, Landbaumeister aus Binz", in: Bundesingenieurkammer (ed.), *Ingenieurbaukunst in Deutschland* [yearbook], Hamburg: Junius, 2001, pp. 134–141.
Holger Barth, "Ulrich Müther", in: Holger Barth / Thomas Topfstedt (ed.), *Vom Baukünstler zum Komplexprojektanten – Architekten in der DDR* [Documentation of an IRS collection of biographic data], (REGIO doc 3 – Document Series), Berlin-Erkner: Institute for Regional Development and Structural Planning, 2000, pp. 162f.

Magazine and newspaper articles

Michael Zajonz, "Ulrich Müther. Bauen wie das Meer", in: *Tagesspiegel*, 08/24/2007, p. 26.

Katinka Corts, "Müthers Freilichtmuseum", in: *tec21*, 2006, No. 6, pp. 5–11.

Uta von Debschitz, "Ostseeperlen", in: *mare. Die Zeitschrift der Meere*, 2003, No. 39, pp. 30–36.

Kai Michel, "Nach der Utopie", in: *brandeins. Wirtschaftsmagazin*, 2003, No. 9, pp. 139–145.

Jürgen Tietz, "Sanierung Teepott", in: *Bauwelt*, 2002, No. 35, p. 2.

Oliver Herwig, "Von Schalen und Segeln", in: *Baumeister – Zeitschrift fürArchitektur*, 2002, No. 12, p. 11.

Carsten Joost, "Hyperbolische Paraboloide. Ulrich Müther, Schalenbaumeister der DDR", in: *Berliner Stadtzeitung Scheinschlag*, 2002, No. 11, p. 9.

Rüdiger Jahnel/Gert König/Gunter Schenck/Nguyen Viet Tue, "Hyparschale Magdeburg", in: *Bautechnik*, 2002, No. 8, pp. 516–522.

Jürgen Tietz, "Swingende Strandarchitektur. Schalenbauten von Ulrich Müther an der Ostseeküste", in: *Neue Zürcher Zeitung*, 08/08/2002, p. 47.

Günther Ackermann, "Der Bau von Schalen für Dachtragwerke aus Stahlbeton im Osten Deutschlands (1945–1985)", in: *Bautechnik*, 2001, No. 1, pp. 18–35.

Kerstin Weinstock, "Ulrich Müther – Vom 'Landbaumeister' zum Schalenbauer", in: *db Deutsche Bauzeitung*, 1999, No. 10, pp. 152–160.

Anne Urbauer, "Müther Superior", in: *Wallpaper*, 1999, No. 24, pp. 73–78.

Andreas Denk, Architektur des 20. Jahrhunderts (44): "Der 'Teepott' von Erich Kaufmann und Ulrich Müther in Rostock-Warnemünde (1968)", in: *Der Architekt. Zeitschrift des Bunds Deutscher Architekten*, 1999, No. 10, p. 14.

Gottfried Hein/Hubert Schlotter, "Das Zeiss-Großplanetarium Berlin im Ernst-Thälmann-Park", in: *Deutsche Architektur*, 1989, No. 10, pp. 9–13.

Dietmar Kuntzsch/Otto Patzelt, "Musikmuschel Saßnitz", in: *Architektur der DDR*, 1989, No. 5, pp. 26f.

Ulrich Müther, "Spritzbeton-Kuppel des Planetariums Wolfsburg", in: *Beton und Stahlbetonbau*, 1985, No. 3, pp. 57–59.

Gertrud Schille, "Planetarium in Wolfsburg", in: *Architektur der DDR*, 1985, No. 1, pp. 37–40.

Ulrich Müther, "Engineering Design and Construction of Doubly Curved Shells for Roof Supporting Structures", in: *IASS, Symposium Spatial Roof Structures*, 1984, pp. 162f.

Gertrud Schille, "Raumflugplanetarium in Tripolis", in: *Architektur der DDR*, 1982, No. 3, pp. 146–153.

Ulrich Müther, "Constructions of Double Curvature Shells for Planetariums", in: *Bulletin of the IASS*, 1979, pp. 49–55.

Arno Claus Martin/Siegfried Fischer, "Mensa der Ingenieurhochschule in Wismar", in: *Architektur der DDR*, 1979, No. 3, pp. 171–173.

Peter Baumbach, "Hauptzentrum Rostock-Evershagen", in: *Architektur der DDR*, 1977, No. 9, pp. 26f.

Erich Kaufmann / Ulrich Müther, "Mehrzweckgaststätte 'Baltic' in Rostock-Lütten Klein", in: *Deutsche Architektur*, 1974, No. 12, pp. 724–726.

Hans-Christian Brümmer, "Gaststättenkomplex in Rostock-Lütten Klein", in: *Deutsche Architektur*, 1973, No. 9, pp. 536–539.

Sieglinde Künzel / Thilo Bunge, "Naherholungszentrum 'Stausee Hohenfelden'", in: *Deutsche Architektur*, 1973, No. 1, pp. 47–49.

Karl Kraus, "Stadthalle Neubrandenburg", in: *Deutsche Architektur*, 1971, No. 6, pp. 351–355.

Wolfgang Reinhard, "Gaststättenkomplex 'Kosmos' im Wohngebietszentrum Rostock-Südstadt", in: *Deutsche Architektur*, 1971, No. 3, pp. 153–158.

Ulrich Müther, "Hypar Shell Construction for Restaurant Teepott in Rostock-Warnemünde, GDR", in: *Bulletin of the IASS*, 1969, pp. 1–12.

Erich Kaufmann / Ulrich Müther, "'Teepott' Rostock-Warnemünde", in: *Deutsche Architektur*, 1969, No. 3, pp. 156–161.

Erich Kaufmann / Ulrich Müther, "Mehrzweckhalle in Rostock-Lütten Klein", in: *Deutsche Architektur*, 1969, No. 2, pp. 80–83.

Erich Kaufmann / Ulrich Müther, "Messehalle in Rostock", in: *Deutsche Architektur*, 1966, No. 11, pp. 676–679.

GDR Architecture Guides

Ingrid Halbach / Matthias Rambow / Horst Büttner / Peter Rätzel, *Architekturführer DDR. Bezirk Frankfurt (Oder)*, Berlin: VEB Verlag für Bauwesen, 1987.

Gudrun Hahn / Serafim Polenz / Heinz Lösler / Heinz Schaeffer / Rudolf Menzel, *Architekturführer DDR, Bezirk Schwerin*, Berlin: VEB Verlag für Bauwesen, 1984.

Walter May / Werner Pampel / Hans Konrad, *Architekturführer DDR. Bezirk Dresden*, Berlin: VEB Verlag für Bauwesen, 1979.

Hans-Otto Möller / Helmut Behrendt / Klaus Marsiske / Ekkehard Franke / Matthias Stahl / Gerd Baier, *Architekturführer DDR. Bezirk Rostock*, Berlin: VEB Verlag für Bauwesen, 1978.

Karl-Heinz Hüter / Siegward Schulrabe / Wilfried Dallmann / Rudolf Zießler, *Architekturführer DDR. Bezirk Erfurt*, Berlin: VEB Verlag für Bauwesen, 1979.

Josef Münzberg / Gerhard Richter / Peter Findeisen, *Architekturführer DDR. Bezirk Halle*, Berlin: VEB Verlag für Bauwesen, 1977.

Joachim Schulz / Wolfgang Müller / Erwin Schrödl, *Architekturführer DDR, Bezirk Leipzig*, Berlin: VEB Verlag für Bauwesen, 1975.

Joachim Schulz / Werner Gräbner, *Architekturführer DDR. Berlin*, Berlin: VEB Verlag für Bauwesen, 1974.

Exhibitions

Kühne Solitäre – die Betonschalen des Ulrich Müther [Travelling exhibition: Künstlerhaus Nürnberg, 2002; Braunschweig, 2002/2003; Technical University Berlin, Schinkel Center for Architecture, 2003; University of Applied Sciences Hildesheim, 2003; Technical University Dresden, 2003, Magdeburg, 2003, Hanover, 2003 among others].

Zwei deutsche Architekturen – 1949 bis 1989, Institute for Foreign Relations e.V. in cooperation with the Federation of German Architecture Collections [Travelling exhibition: Kunsthaus Hamburg, 2004; Fair Palace Municipal Department Store, Leipzig, 2004; Technical University Delft, 2005; Technical University Istanbul, 2005; National Museum for Contemporary Art, Bucharest, 2006; Megaron Athens, 2006; Royal Museum for Art and History, Brussels, 2007; Royal Danish Art Academy, Copenhagen, 2007; Antiguo Convento Santa María de los Reyes, Sevilla, 2007; Diputación de Málaga, Málaga, 2008; Museo de Bellas Artes, A Coruña, 2008; Pamplona City Hall, 2008; Arquería de los Nuevos Ministerios, Madrid, 2008].

Kühne Solitäre – Baukunst statt Plattenbau. Die Hyparschalen des Baumeisters Ulrich Müther [Exhibition: Multi-Cultural Center of Templin, Templin, 2006].

Hypar. Modelle, Zeichnungen und Dokumentation [Exhibition in the Gallery of the County of Rügen, Putbus, 2007].

Film

Für den Schwung sind Sie zuständig (It's Up to You to Make it Swing), Documentary film, 58 min., book and direction: Margarete Fuchs, produced in 2002, first showing in 2006.

Archive

Müther Archive, Faculty of Design, College of Wismar

The collection of documents includes the entire estate of Ulrich Müther's architectural activity in the form of plans, photos, models, administrative documents and various files.

Imprint and Thanks

Concept, texts, design, typesetting and plans Rahel Lämmler, Michael Wagner

Blueprint research Müther-Archive, College of Wismar

Translation German/English Geoffrey Steinherz, Lynnette Widder

Proof Reading Christina Bösel, Kerstin Forster

Lithography and printing Heer Druck AG, Sulgen

Binding Buchbinderei Scherrer AG, Urdorf

Photography Dominic Ott, Zurich [except: pp. 18f. Instituto Técnico de la Construcción y del Cemento, Sección Fotografía; p. 23 from: Ekkehard Schramm/Eberhard Schunck, *Heinz Isler Schalen*; pp. 24–26 from: Colin Faber, *Candela - The Shell Builder*; p. 28 from: Jürgen Joedicke, *Schalenbau*; p. 38 Michael Wagner; p. 41 Darr, p. 45 Mohr, Bild und Heimat Verlag; p. 69 Lutz Grünke; pp. 5f., pp. 8–14, p. 31, p. 34, pp. 107–112 Müther Archive; p. 63 Rahel Lämmler; p. 110 Jena, p. 111 Berlin, Carl Zeiss Archive]

The publisher and the authors have done their best to acquire the necessary rights of reproduction for all illustrations. In the case that we have missed something, we excuse ourselves and will welcome being informed about our oversight.

The German edition "Ulrich Müther Schalenbauten" was published in 2008 and since reprinted twice.

© 2010 by Verlag Niggli AG, Sulgen | Zürich, www.niggli.ch
as well as the authors and photographers
ISBN 978-3-7212-0747-7

We would like to thank all who contributed to the creation of this publication including:

Dominic Ott, Marianne Wagner, Fabienne Lämmler, Theres Hollenstein, Erik Marokko, Marc Munter, Massimo Laffranchi

Astrid von Zydowitz-Müther, Lutz Grünke, Dietrich Otto, Christoph Weinhold, Winfried Jax, Dieter Mathis, Malte Preuhs, Jana Hartwig, the Carl Zeiss Archive, the Catholic Rectory of Neubrandenburg, the University Archive of the Technical University of Dresden, the municipal archives and historic preservation and building authorities of Neubrandenburg, Rostock, Bergen, Schwerin and Stralsund

For their generous support we also thank the following firms and institutions:

GERDA HENKEL **STIFTUNG**

Society for Civil Engineering, Switzerland

Cultural Foundation of Rügen

 RIEDER [fibre C]

Cover photo Lifeguard Rescue Tower 2, Beach Promenade Binz, 1981